ST. GEORGE AND THE PYGMIES

*The Story of
Tsuga Canadensis 'Minuta'*

by

PETER DEL TREDICI

*ARNOLD ARBORETUM
JAMAICA PLAIN
MASSACHUSETTS*

Theophrastus

LITTLE COMPTON, RHODE ISLAND

Library of Congress Cataloging in Publication Data

Del Tredici, Peter, 1945–
  St. George and the pygmies.

  Bibliography: p.
  1. Eastern hemlock—Varieties. 2. Dwarf conifers—
Varieties. 3. St. George, Daniel M., 1890–1983.
4. Plant collectors—Vermont—Biography. I. Title.
II. Title: Saint George and the pygmies.
SB413.E27D45   1984   634.9′753   84-8909
ISBN 0-913728-35-7 (pbk.)

*To
Gus Kelley
whose persistence knows no bounds*

*To Brother David
from little
brother
- Peter*

CONTENTS

	Preface	7
1	Vermont Idyll	9
2	'Minuta'	15
3	'Abbott's Pigmy Hemlock'	23
4	'Pygmaea'	32
5	Summary	39
6	Nomenclature	41
7	St. George	44
	Bibliography	47

PREFACE

When people ask me how I could possibly write a whole book about a single cultivar, I usually shrug my shoulders and answer, "Because it's a very interesting plant." But this is hardly a legitimate response, since all plants—from the majestic redwoods to the lowly ragweed—are interesting and deserve to have books written about them.

Tsuga canadensis 'Minuta' is the subject of the present work not only because it is worthy, but also because its history is badly in need of review. Indeed, my researches clearly show that the traditional story of the plant's origin is built upon a foundation of contradictions that cannot bear the weight of facts. Hopefully, this work will not only rebuild that history, but will also clarify the nomenclatural muddle that has plagued this little green gem since its introduction in 1935.

If all this sounds like a familiar story to the reader, I can only say that it should, because it is very similar to the one I described for Sargent's weeping hemlock in *A Giant Among The Dwarfs*. No doubt, future research will show that the same story applies to a great many other important garden plants.

At this time, I would like to thank Ricardo Austrich of Cornell University, Harold Epstein of Larchmont, New York, and Joel Spingarn of Baldwin, New York, for their cooperation with this project. I would also like to thank the entire staff of the Arnold Arboretum for putting up with yet another hemlock odyssey.

Peter Del Tredici
29 March 1984

1

Vermont Idyll

To people interested in dwarf conifers, the name Daniel M. St. George stands out like a beacon—the man who discovered *Tsuga canadensis* 'Minuta', the miniature Canadian hemlock. This plant is a true genetic dwarf, growing slowly and reliably year in, year out, never more than an inch a season, and usually half as much. It doesn't suddenly bolt as many dwarfs do, and it doesn't thin out and become leggy. Indeed, the oldest documented specimen of 'Minuta', after more than 40 years of cultivation, is still only 18 inches high and 22 inches wide—a perfect pincushion of a plant.

The history of 'Minuta', like that of many horticultural gems, is shrouded in confusion. The plant was first brought to public attention in 1935, by Henry Teuscher of the New York Botanical Garden. In an article that appeared in an English periodical, *The New Flora and Silva,* he presented an incredible story:

> It was discovered in 1927 in an out-of-the-way part of the so-called Green Mountains,

from which the state of Vermont derives its name (Ver mont—Green mountain). These mountains are a northerly extension of the great Appalachian system that forms the eastern highland of North America. The old plant which was found there was only about two feet tall and as much in diameter, but it held some old cones on its tiny branchlets. It was evident that an attempt to dig up and to transport this old plant would result in its destruction because of the nature of the locality; so it was left undisturbed and is still there, having been seen by only one man who refuses to divulge its exact whereabouts. But the finder brought back with him several young seedlings which he gathered near the old plant, and of which the picture shows one (figure 1). Returning to the same place several times during the last eight years, he collected altogether some 25 seedlings, of which all are dwarf and show surprisingly little variation.

The discoverer, who is very secretive about the details of his find, so far could not be prevailed upon to make a special trip in the fall in order to gather seeds. He claims that the place is very difficult to reach, and that only in the spring, after the snow of the winter has matted down the leaves, and after the tall ferns which abound there are gone, is it possible to find the tiny seedlings. It appears to be beyond doubt that this plant is a true dwarf, not a witchbroom like most of

FIGURE 1. Tsuga canadensis minuta. *Photo published by Henry Teuscher in* The New Flora and Sylva, *1935. Reproduced here life size in a strawberry box.*

the dwarf conifers in cultivation, and that its low stature is to a surprising degree inherited by its offspring. The writer's attention was called to this interesting variety by Mr.

11

George Ehrle, nurseryman of Richfield, New Jersey, who has interested himself for many years in the forms of *Tsuga canadensis*, of which some 30 are represented in his collection (pp. 274–275).

It is significant that Teuscher does not provide the name of the person who discovered the plant. He only says that George Ehrle called it to his attention. It was John C. Swartley who credited Daniel St. George with the discovery of 'Minuta' in his unpublished Cornell University master's degree thesis of 1939, "Canada Hemlock and Its Variations". Under the section on variety *minuta*, he describes Ehrle's plant as follows:

> Type Plant: (Plant No. 1529, 15 × 15 cm. (6" × 6"), 6/22/38. No herbarium specimen collected.) Irregular in outline and very compact with short crowded branchlets; annual growth about 1–2 cm. (2/5–4/5 in.); leaves mostly supraplanate, linear, obtuse at the apex, shorter and more crowded than normal hemlock and medium green in color.
>
> This plant which is probably 25–35 years old, was collected near Charlotte, Chittenden County, Vermont, and is now growing in the rock garden of George L. Ehrle, Clifton, New Jersey. The following story has been gleaned from correspondence between Mr. Ehrle and Daniel M. St. George of Charlotte, Vermont, the finder of this interesting strain of Canadian hemlock.
>
> Several years ago, a Mr. Craig informed

Mr. Ehrle of the existence of this very dwarf strain and Mr. Ehrle at once investigated the possibility of acquiring a specimen. He was informed that there were two plants available at five dollars each so he quickly ordered these and they were received September 10, 1934. Mr. St. George reported that they had been dug in 1927 on a north slope of the Green Mountains, at a rather high altitude in a small open area with normal hemlock growing on all sides. Mr. St. George dug some small plants in 1931. In September 1934, he again visited the site to collect another lot of plants and found the parent which was about two feet high and very dense, just like the small ones. It was standing beside a maple tree, crowded on one side by a spruce, but it was bearing cones and seedlings were distributed within 45 m. (150 ft.). This plant must have been more than 50 years old. In the spring of 1935, another visit was made but the place had been so closely grazed by cattle that not a single plant exactly like the others could be found and even the parent was dead. However, Mr. St. George reported digging two faster-growing plants 1.2 m (4 ft.) high and observing several more with similar foliage.

Mr. St. George transplanted all of these dwarf hemlocks to his small nursery, shading them only the first year. He stated that they were easy to establish and very hardy. Altogether he dug and sold 25 to 30 plants,

> but with the exception of Mr. Ehrle, he has no record of the identity of his customers.
>
> Mr. Ehrle used one of the small plants to supply scions for grafting, but without success. The other plant (No. 1529) is not thriving, but some cuttings have been successfully rooted by Mr. Ehrle; therefore this strain will not be lost. This plant was used by Teuscher in describing var. *minuta*; therefore it is unquestionably the type plant of that variety (pp. 261–263).

Since Swartley's thesis was never published, St. George's role as discoverer was not widely recognized until 1965 when an excerpt from it was printed in Den Ouden and Boom's *Manual of Cultivated Conifers*. In that same year, J. E. Spingarn also excerpted Swartley's thesis for an article on Canadian hemlock varieties that he wrote for *American Horticultural Magazine*. Time however does not stand still, and in the almost 30 years that intervened between the thesis completion and the publication of its two excerpts, the botany and history of 'Minuta' became unbelievably entangled with that of two other very similar plants—'Abbott's Pigmy Hemlock' and 'Pygmaea'. Interestingly, it was Swartley himself, and his mentor, C. F. Jenkins, the founder of the Hemlock Arboretum, who initiated the confusion by publishing several different versions of the discovery of these three plants. It was in the light of this confusion that I undertook my own study of 'Minuta' in 1981.

2

'Minuta'

Starting my researches at the most obvious place, I contacted directory assistance for Charlotte and got the number of the only St. George in the book, Alma, whom I called up. To my utter amazement, she told me that, yes, uncle Dan was still alive and that, yes, he still had three of his dwarf hemlocks growing in his front yard. I could scarcely believe it—three original specimens of 'Minuta' still alive along with their discoverer. I immediately made preparations for a trip to visit St. George.

I arrived in Charlotte, on the shores of Lake Champlaign, on April 11, 1981, and, tape recorder in hand, made my way to Dan's house. At last I was going to meet the man who had discovered 'Minuta'—the one person who could clear up the history of the plant. I even fantasized that perhaps St. George would be willing to sell one of his plants to the Arnold Arboretum. With all these thoughts running through my head, I was completely taken by surprise when St. George asked me if I had seen the plants when I drove in. "No," I answered, "I didn't." So he took me out front to show me his hemlocks, and to my utter disbelief, they weren't 'Minuta' at all. There were two sparsely branched plants about eight feet tall and one perfect pyramid, ten feet tall. This pyramid was clearly a beautiful plant, but it was just as clearly not 'Minuta'. My heart sank and, try as I might, I could not really give his plants the enthusiasm they deserved (figure 2).

We went inside Dan's little house and I attempted to pull myself together. "What about 'Minuta'?" I asked. "I thought you discovered 'Minuta'." He didn't know what I meant by 'Minuta', so I showed him the picture from Teuscher's 1935 article. He looked it over carefully before handing it back to me. No, he never found anything that looked like that. Of all the dwarf hemlocks he discovered—and he said there were 14 in all—13 were sparse and narrow like the two in his yard, and the fourteenth was the dense pyramid that was also in the yard. He had not collected them in Charlotte, he insisted, but in Richmond, about 15 miles away. In disbelief, I pressed him further, but he stuck to his story. In 1928, he was out collecting with his partner, Larry Root, near the Winooski River in Richmond, when the plug fell out of the gas tank of their car and they had to stop.

"Well, we went out the next day. We still had an order for a lot of hemlocks. Course I'd traveled that road and I'd seen these hemlocks up in there. I told Larry, I says, we go up in there and see if there's anything. Got to walking around, stepped on one of these and it flopped me over. I reached down in the moss, pulled it and it come up easy."

As Dan described it, they were in a wet area and he didn't see the plants until he literally stumbled on them. They were growing right in the moss and looked just like part of it.

FIGURE 2. *Daniel M. St. George with the dense pyramidal hemlock he collected in Richmond, Vermont, in 1932. The plant is ten feet tall. Photo by P. Del Tredici, 1981.*

ST. GEORGE AND THE PYGMIES

"Did you ever find the parent plant of all the seedlings?" I asked him.

His answer was brutally frank: "When we was up there, there was a lot of hemlocks that was cut down. I suppose that's where the seed come from—some of them hemlocks. But they was all cut off by the time we got there. Just lots of moss."[1]

The actual site as St. George described it was on the east side of the Winooski River in Richmond, where Route 2 crosses over an iron bridge. Near this bridge he said is a "checkered house"—which is still there—and behind this house was where he found his plants.[2]

On this day, back in 1928, said St. George, he and Larry Root took 13 narrow plants from this site; 11 were small and two were big. These two big ones, which he planted in his yard, have grown up to become the sparsely branched plants still alive today (figure 3). In 1932 he went back to the site and dug a fourteenth plant that was different from the ones he had collected in 1928. It was three feet tall with a trunk two inches in diameter and very dense in its growth. He planted this plant in his yard—it is now the pyramid—along with the two sparse plants from

---

[1] It should be noted here that moss makes an ideal seed bed for many plants. Guy Nearing noted this fact for rhododendrons in 1957, and I'm certain it also holds true for hemlocks: "Anyone who had wandered through wild stands of *Rhododendron maximum* and *Kalmia latifolia* must have noticed how thousands of seedlings spring up, not among the fallen forest leaves, nor yet on bare ground, but chiefly among moss-covered mounds and banks." (p. 197)

[2] After interviewing St. George, I went to the checkered house and looked around. All the land was closely grazed by cattle and a new interchange for Interstate Highway 89 had drastically altered the landscape. Needless to say, I didn't find any dwarf hemlocks.

FIGURE 3. *The two sparsely branched hemlocks discovered by Daniel St. George in 1928. The plants are eight feet tall. Photo by P. Del Tredici, 1981.*

his 1928 collection. In 1934, he sold one of his discoveries to J. Watson Webb, a railroad man from Shelburne, Vermont, who planted it on his estate on Long Island, New York. The other ten he sold to C. F. Jenkins of the Hemlock Arboretum in Germantown, Pennsylvania, for $100. I was surprised by this bit of information because Jenkins, who usually acknowledged the contributions of others, *never* mentioned St. George in any of the *Hemlock Arboretum Bulletins* that he published quarterly between 1932 and 1951. According to Dan, Jenkins sent him a stack of letters asking for more plants and information, but he never answered any of them. St. George also said that the only other person, besides Larry Root, whom he told about the Winooski River discovery site was his good friend, Fred Abbey of North Farrisburg, Vermont, who, like St. George, was a breeder and grower of lilies. St. George denied knowing anyone named George Ehrle or ever writing to him. He did, however, say he knew Mr. Craig, the man whom Swartley credits with telling George Ehrle about the existence of the dwarf hemlocks. According to St. George, Mr. Craig also worked with lilies. My own researches have uncovered the fact that Craig was from Wayland, Massachusetts, and a good friend of Fred Abbey's (see Yerex, 1961, and Abbey, 1967).

So lilies seem to be the glue that holds the 'Minuta' story together. St. George was a breeder of lilies. He told another breeder, Fred Abbey, about the site and he, I suspect, told his good friend and fellow lily fancier, William N. Craig, about it. It was Mr. Craig who told George Ehrle about the plants and George Ehrle who told Harry Teuscher. The whole story hangs together beautifully except for the fact that St. George denied ever finding a plant that looked like 'Minuta'.

'MINUTA'

In comparing the Teuscher/Swartley version with St. George's own story, the differences are readily apparent. However, there are some similarities—such as that between the alleged parent plant and St. George's dense pyramid. Indeed, I suspect that the Teuscher/Swartley story is basically the St. George story, modified and embellished by virtue of having been retold several times. It is like the children's game "Telephone", where one person whispers something to the person next to him, who tells it to the next person, who in turn tells it to the next, and so on and so forth around the room. What comes out at the end usually bears little resemblance to what went in at the beginning.

While it is possible that St. George's memory could have become clouded during the more than 50 years that elapsed between the actual discovery of the plants and my interview with him, the three non-'Minuta' hemlocks in his front yard provide hard evidence to the contrary. Indeed, the fact that St. George adamantly denied knowing Ehrle or ever writing to him raises serious questions about the nature of the "correspondence" between them from which Swartley "gleaned" his story—questions which are accentuated by the fact that Swartley, by his own admission, never visited St. George when he was writing his thesis. If actual letters had been exchanged between Ehrle and St. George, one would expect Teuscher to have credited St. George with the discovery of 'Minuta', as Swartley did. This inconsistency, in conjunction with several others of less significance, suggests to me that both authors based their stories not on conversations with or letters from St. George but on conversations with or letters from George Ehrle. To put it another way, the commonly accepted 'Minuta' story is hearsay. It is not supported by any written evidence, and it is not corroborated by the central witness.

The question still remains, of course, as to who the real discoverer of 'Minuta' was. Unfortunately my own researches have failed to provide an answer. Quite literally, it could have been *anyone* who talked to Daniel St. George, Larry Root or Fred Abbey about the Richmond hemlocks. The fact that C. F. Jenkins of Philadelphia purchased some of the plants in 1934 shows just how far the hemlock grapevine stretched.

Regardless of who the discoverer of 'Minuta' was, it seems likely that he found the plant near the Richmond site that St. George discovered in 1928. It also seems likely that this person did not want people to know that he had raided St. George's spot and, therefore, kept his identity secret.

3

'Abbott's Pigmy Hemlock'

If the 'Minuta' story were to end here, it would be confusing enough, but it goes on and on and on. When I was checking C. F. Jenkins's *Hemlock Arboretum Bulletins,* the following entry from #5, October 1933, leapt out at me: "Mr. Abbott has grafted plants of all of these growing in his trial grounds. His so-called No. 4 was a dwarf pincushion which he had gathered on the hills on the south bank of the Winooski River, in Richmond, Chittenden County. We spent a glorious afternoon [September 30] tramping over this region hoping to find others of this diminutive type." Incredible as it seems, Abbott and Jenkins were out looking for dwarf hemlocks in 1933 in the exact spot where St. George had found his plants in 1928. Indeed, this was the *second* time Abbott had been there. To say that this was just coincidence strains credulity. It makes more sense to assume that Abbott heard about St. George's find through the plant collector's grapevine and went up to Richmond to check out the location.

In the next *Bulletin,* January 1934, Jenkins makes it clear that his collecting efforts in September were not in vain: "Frank L. Abbott and I found two wild seedlings along the Winooski River in Vermont. Mr. Abbott really discovered them." He then lists one of these plants under accession "No. 21. *Tsuga canadensis* var. *pygmaeus*. Hort. A seedling found along the Winooski River, Vermont. Resembling *T. canadensis* var. *macrophylla*. Rehder."

The matter rested here until 1939, when John Swartley completed his thesis, "Canada Hemlock and Its Variations." In this work, he described no fewer than 21 botanical varieties, each with a type plant on which the description was based and several variant plants that were similar enough to the type to receive the same classification. Under variety *minuta*, Swartley used Ehrle's plant as the type and went on to list an additional ten variants. These plants came from all over the northeast and ranged in size from six inches by six inches (Ehrle's plant) to four feet two inches by five feet four inches (a plant at the Durand Eastman Park in Rochester, New York). Among the variants was a plant in Abbott's garden in Vermont:

> Variant No. 1 (Plant No. 1349 (A5) 24 × 17 cm. (9½" × 6½") 6/26/38. No herbarium specimen collected.) Very similar to the type plant although the leaves are more nearly biplanate. This plant has grown about 9 cm. (3½ in.) in 5 years.

FIGURE 4. *A definition of terms as it appeared in John Swartley's 1939 Master's Degree thesis,* Canada Hemlock and its Variations. *These terms were invented by Swartley.*

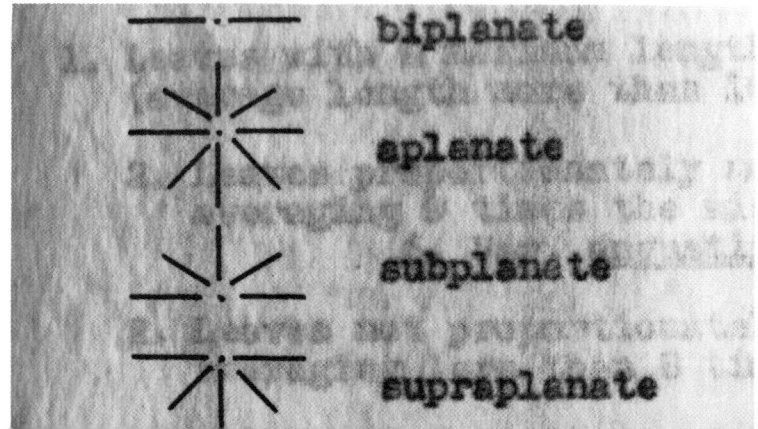

FIGURE 5. *This illustration is copied from Mr. Swartley's thesis. The caption reads: "Variant No. 1. Plant No. 1349. Seedling at Athens, Vermont, collected near Richmond, Vermont." Note that the needles are clearly arranged in a single plane.*

No. 1349 and another similar plant which has since died were collected by Frank L. Abbott in May 1933, north of Richmond, Chittenden County, Vermont, on the west side of the Winooski River on the same ridge of mountains as No. 1529 (George Ehrle's plant) and only about 16 km. (10 mi.) away. Mr. Abbott has grafted this variant and one of the small grafted plants (No. J121) is growing at Far Country (p. 263).

Since the plant was found in May 1933, it cannot be one of the ones that Abbott found when he was out tramping around with Jenkins in September of that same year. It must be Abbott's No. 4—the "dwarf pincushion" that Jenkins referred to in *Bulletin #5*.

In his thesis, Swartley makes it very clear that Abbott's plant is distinguishable from 'Minuta' by virtue of the fact that its needles are arranged in a single plane (biplanate), not radially around half the stem (supraplanate) (figure 4). The two plants are totally different. The picture that he provided of Abbott's plant further substantiated its distinctiveness from 'Minuta' (figure 5).

In 1942, Swartley attempted to make the material in his thesis more useful to horticulturists by publishing a short article in *Standardized Plant Names*. In this book, under the *Tsuga* entry, he gave names to some of the plants that were identified in his thesis by numbers. One such plant was variant No. 1 of the thesis (#1349), growing in Abbott's garden, which he chose to call "ABBOTT PYGMY." Remarkably, he arbitrarily changed the name of George Ehrle's plant (#1529) to "CHARLOTTE PYGMY." Nowhere in the article does he refer to 'Minuta' or to Daniel St. George. While these new name assignments are interesting and well intended, they only served to further confuse the situation since the thesis descriptions upon which they were based were never published.

The valid naming of Abbott's curious little plant did not come until 1948 when C. F. Jenkins wrote an article titled "The Dwarfest of the Dwarfs" (*Bulletin* #62) in which he called it 'Abbott's Pigmy Hemlock' and classified it under *Tsuga canadensis* var. *minuta,* as Swartley had done in his thesis. According to Jenkins, the plant was discovered by Frank Abbott in Richmond, Vermont, in 1933, and in 1938 a grafted propagation of it was sent to the Hemlock Arboretum. The distinguishing feature of this plant, he said, was that it grew very slowly, having increased only 3½ inches in height and 5½ inches in width after ten years.[3] Unfortunately, Jenkins made one error in his article which greatly confused an already complicated situation—he printed a picture of Henry Teuscher's straw-

---

[3]This slow growth rate of Jenkins's grafted propagation is only half that of the mother plant in Abbott's garden which, according to Swartley's thesis, grew 3½ inches in five years.

Abbott's Pigmy Hemlock. Tsuga canadensis minuta.
Arriving in a strawberry box.
Photo. by John C. Swartley

FIGURE 6. *George Ehrle's 'Minuta' misidentified as 'Abbott's Pigmy Hemlock' by C. F. Jenkins in* Hemlock Arboretum Bulletin #62, 1948. *This is the same plant that is shown in figure 1. Only the position of the slip of paper and the ruler are different.*

berry box 'Minuta' and called it 'Abbott's Pigmy Hemlock' (figure 6).

In the next Bulletin, Jenkins owned up to his misidentification, but neglected to do the one thing that would really clear up the confusion—publish a picture of the real 'Abbott's Pigmy Hemlock'. Why he did not will never be known, but in this same article he gives what I'm sure he hoped would be the last word on Abbott's mysterious plant:

> In the April Hemlock Bulletin (No. 62), an illustration was shown of a very dwarf hemlock in a strawberry box and labelled "Abbott's Pigmy Hemlock". My old friend, George L. Ehrle of Clifton, N.J., to whom we are indebted for many of the specimens in the Arboretum, calls attention to the fact that we were in error regarding the name and the illustration. Actually, the photograph from which the illustration was made was taken by or for Henry Teuscher, now curator of the Montreal Botanical Garden. Mr. Teuscher first named and described *Tsuga canadensis* var. *minuta* in "New Flora and Sylva", Vol. VII, No. 4, p. 274, July, 1935.

(There then follows a lengthy quote from Teuscher's article, after which Jenkins begins again.)

> Several years ago, a Mr. Craig informed Mr. Ehrle of the existence of this very dwarf plant and Mr. Ehrle at once investigated the possibility of acquiring a specimen. He was informed that there were two plants available, so he quickly ordered these and they were received September 10, 1934.
> The little dwarf growing in the Hemlock Arboretum was a gift from Frank L. Abbott

'ABBOTT'S PIGMY HEMLOCK'

of Saxton's River, Vt. It is a grafted plant from one collected by him in May 1933, north of Richmond, Chittenden County, Vermont, on the west side of the Winooski River, on the same ridge of mountains as the little plants described by Mr. Teuscher which were found near Charlotte in the same county. According to the map Charlotte and Richmond are about fifteen miles apart as the proverbial Vermont crow would fly. Mr. Abbott found two plants from one of which the dwarf at "Far Country" was propagated.

At the time John C. Swartley prepared his thesis, "Canada Hemlock and its Variations", the taxonomic authorities at Cornell University condoned the practice of applying one Latin, varietal name to a complex of different clones that closely resembled each other. Accordingly the dwarf plant from Mr. Abbott was labelled var. *minuta* in that time and the label has never been changed. Correctly, a varietal name, whether it be Latin or vernacular, should apply only to one individual and its progeny. The Abbott Pigmy Hemlock is very similar to var. *minuta* but has a slightly different foliage character. Its leaves do not diverge quite so much from the axis of the branchlets. But the companion plant collected by Mr. Abbott is so like var. *minuta* that we challenge anyone to find any distinction between them. This original plant is growing in Mr. Abbott's garden in Vermont. Although in perfect health, the increase in height over a period of 15 years was less than 4 inches. The cooperation of John C. Swartley, the hemlock expert, was secured in preparing this explanation and correction.

This description of 'Abbott's Pigmy Hemlock' matches that of variant No. 1 (plant #1349) in Swartley's master's thesis. Both refer to a plant found in Richmond, Vermont, in May, 1933, that was distinguishable from 'Minuta' by virtue of the fact that its needles are arranged, not radially around the stem, but in a single plane. As Swartley indicated in *Standardized Plant Names*, 'Abbott's Pigmy Hemlock' and variant No. 1 are one and the same plant.

As for the 'Abbott's Pigmy' companion, there is no such agreement between the thesis and *Hemlock Arboretum Bulletin* #63. In 1939 Swartley stated flatly that the plant was dead. In 1948, he said it was alive and well and looked just like 'Minuta'. In the absence of any explanation, the whole thing looks a bit like a shell game with a hemlock instead of a pea.

It is also worth noting that Jenkins and Swartley make no mention of Daniel St. George in their article. This is rather strange in view of the fact that Swartley so definitely credited him with the discovery of 'Minuta' in his 1939 thesis. Could it be that Swartley had second thoughts about St. George's role? Or was he left out simply to save space? I rather doubt this latter possibility given that Mr. Craig is mentioned, along with St. George's home town of Charlotte and the date on which Ehrle received the plants. No, I feel certain that if Swartley had known who discovered 'Minuta', he would have come right out and said so in this supposedly definitive article. The fact that he doesn't strongly suggests that he had doubts about his earlier assertion that St. George found the plant—doubts which my own researches have clearly substantiated.

Amidst all the contradictions, resurrections, omissions and mislabeled photographs, it's easy to see how people could start getting confused. Henry Teuscher was one such person. He saw Jenkins's article in *Bulletin* #62 and, in 1949, published one of his own in *Plants and Gardens* proclaiming Frank Abbott the discoverer of the plant that he had described as var. *minuta* in 1935. To top this off, he printed a picture of his original var. *minuta* and labeled it 'Abbott's Pigmy Hemlock' just as Jenkins had done a year earlier. Thus it was that 'Minuta' was transformed into 'Abbott's Pigmy Hemlock'—a transformation that has taken some thirty-five years to disentangle. It's a sad fact that all this ridiculous confusion could have been avoided had either Swartley or Jenkins taken the trouble to review their earlier writings on the subject.

4

'Pygmaea'

As far as I could determine, *Tsuga canadensis* 'Pygmaea' was first described by Harold Hillier in *Dwarf Conifers* in 1964: "Short congested annual growths, leaves typical" (p. 66). In 1966, Humphrey Welch expanded the description by noting that "'Pygmaea' is very similar in habit and growth [to 'Minuta'], except that it may be even smaller and have shorter leaves" (p. 321).

In 1969, Joel Spingarn provided an illustration of 'Pygmaea' and gave its full history:

> I raised the plant from a single cutting generously supplied by Mr. William Gotelli. I have attempted to trace the origin of this form. Mr. Gotelli's plant [see figure 7] was obtained from Mr. Henry Hohman of Kingsville Nursery, who raised the plant from a single scion supplied by Mr. Joseph Gable of Stewartstown, Pa., in 1941. I have been unable to contact Mr. Gable, so there the search ends; however, Mr. John C. Swartley wrote

FIGURE 7. Tsuga canadensis pygmaea *photographed at the Gotelli Arboretum, South Orange, N.J., probably in 1961. Arnold Arboretum Archives.*

that the form *T. can.* 'Pygmaea' is similar to form *T. can.* 'Minuta', the latter having slightly longer leaves. His inference, I believe, is that the form 'Pygmaea' is one of the seedlings of *T. can.* 'Minuta' collected at the site of the parent plant discovered in Charlotte, Vermont (p. 88).

Clearly the history of 'Pygmaea' is just as vague and confused as that of 'Minuta' and 'Abbott's Pigmy Hemlock'. When one is faced with such uncertainty, the appropriate response is to go back to original sources. Happily, Swartley's earlier writings are more enlightening than his speculation quoted by Spingarn. In 1946, in an article about hemlocks that appeared in *American Nurseryman,* he presented a plant that could well be 'Pygmaea':

> Probably the most interesting plant in Mr. Abbott's collection is a dwarf, apparently identical to the one that has been propagated by George L. Ehrle and described by Henry Teuscher as var. *minuta.* It is exactly one foot high, perfectly healthy and at least 35 years old. It is the largest existing plant of this type that is known. Harold Epstein wrote that he has a small plant that he obtained from Mr. Ehrle. Does anyone else have one? Of course, such a slow-growing plant is not practical commercially (p. 8).

In 1948, in *The Hemlock Arboretum Bulletin* #63, Jenkins and Swartley gave a fuller history of Abbott's 'Minuta' look-alike: "But the companion plant [to 'Abbott's Pigmy Hemlock'] collected by Mr. Abbott is so like var. *minuta* that we challenge anyone to find any distinction between them. This original plant is growing in Mr. Abbott's garden in Vermont."

Ignoring the fact that this statement contradicts Swartley's thesis assertion that the original companion plant died before 1939, this resurrected companion plant could easily be 'Pygmaea', especially when one remembers that in 1933 Jenkins classified the dwarf hemlock that Abbott found in Richmond, Vermont, as var. *pygmaeus.* Certainly it makes more sense to postulate a nurseryman

'PYGMAEA'

like Joe Gable taking cuttings from Abbott's well publicized plant and later distributing them as 'Pygmaea', than it does to postulate the existence of a new sibling of 'Minuta' that went undescribed for thirty years. (Of course, this is not to say that 'Pygmaea', as the resurrected companion, might not be a sibling of 'Minuta'.)

In his 1969 article, Spingarn clearly takes up the Jenkins/Swartley challenge to find a difference between 'Minuta' and 'Pygmaea':

> Mr. Swartley also suggests that the growth rates are apparently the same, and I suppose this would be correct if one were to consider that the difference in growth rate is only a fraction of an inch; however, upon actually taking measurements I found the form 'Minuta' grows ⅜" on the shortest shoots and up to ¾" on the longest shoots while the form 'Pygmaea' measures ⅛" on the shortest shoots to ⅜" on the longest shoots, so, relatively speaking, if we were to strike an average, the form 'Minuta' grows twice the rate of 'Pygmaea'! Both plants measured are well established and growing on the same site (p. 88).

While I do not question the accuracy of Spingarn's measurements, I feel that by themselves, they are not adequate to differentiate the two plants. As everyone who gardens knows, growth rate is greatly influenced by environmental factors such as planting in the sun versus shade and propagation by grafting versus cuttings. It is also undeniable that the abundance of moisture, the condition of the soil and the frequency of transplanting can all have measurable effects on growth rate.

In 1969, Spingarn's 'Pygmaea' was 4 inches high and 6.5 inches wide. When A. M. Kelley of Little Compton, R.I., measured it in 1983, it was 12 inches high and 18.5 inches wide. This is an increase in growth of 0.6 inches a year in height and 0.9 inches a year in width—substantially greater than the 0.1 to 0.4 inches a year that Spingarn originally reported for the plant. It is interesting to compare these figures with those obtained from Harold Epstein's 'Minuta' (figure 8 on page 38). This plant is used for comparison because, as Swartley pointed out in 1946, it is a propagation of George Ehrle's original 'Minuta'. In 1983, Harold's plant was 18 inches high and 22 inches across. Assuming that all this growth was made after 1946 (which is clearly not the case) one gets an annual increase in height of 0.5 inches and increase in width of 0.6 inches. Harold Epstein's 'Minuta' then, is a slower grower than Spingarn's 'Pygmaea' in both dimensions. The point of these measurements, however, is not just to show that one

Table 1: Growth Rates of 'Minuta' and 'Pygmaea' at the Arnold Arboretum—1962–1983.

NAME	NUMBER	SOURCE	MODE OF PROPAGATION
'Minuta'	1068–62	Hohman	Graft
'Minuta'	1763–65	Hillier	Rooted Cutting
'Minuta'	1497–71	1763-65	Rooted Cutting
'Pygmaea'	955-70	Spingarn	Rooted Cutting
'Pygmaea'	1068-71	Hillier	Rooted Cutting (?)

'PYGMAEA'

plant is faster or slower than another, but that growth rate *by itself* is not a characteristic that one can use to separate different cultivars. This assertion is supported by my own observations on the growth rates of specimens of 'Minuta' and 'Pygmaea' growing at the Arnold Arboretum (Table 1).

The slowest grower by far is the 'Minuta' from Henry Hohman. In addition, the average rates of increase for 'Minuta' are less than for 'Pygmaea'. When one excludes Hohman's 'Minuta' from the calculations, because it is grafted and growing in the shade, the growth rates of the two cultivars are the same for the width increase and different by only 0.1 inch for height. At the Arnold Arboretum, then, 'Minuta' and 'Pygmaea' grow at basically the same rate.

I could also find no support for the assertion that 'Pygmaea' has smaller leaves than 'Minuta'. In measuring 25 of the normal sized needles from the elongated stems immediately below the congested shoot tips, the needle length of 'Pygmaea' (Spingarn) was 0.30 inches, while for

	Height	Width
Average Yearly Growth of 3 specimens of 'Minuta':	0.8"	1.1"
Average Yearly Growth of 2 specimens of 'Pygmaea':	0.8"	1.2"

INITIAL SIZE WHEN RECEIVED	—1983— HEIGHT	WIDTH	YEARLY INC. HEIGHT	WIDTH	SITE
2½" — 1962	13"	21"	.5	.9	Shade
2" — 1965	18"	23"	.9	1.2	Sun
1" — 1972	12"	15"	1.0	1.3	Sun
1" — 1970	12"	17"	.8	1.2	Sun
4" — 1971	15"	20"	.9	1.3	Sun

'Minuta' (Hillier) it was 0.29 inches. On the congested shoot tips themselves, there was so much variability on each cultivar that comparative measurements between cultivars were impossible.

Clearly needle length, like growth rate, is not a distinct enough character to allow one to distinguish 'Minuta' from 'Pygmaea'. Indeed, I seriously doubt whether there is any morphological feature on which a valid separation of the two plants can be based. I don't even think it can be conclusively proven that 'Pygmaea' is not 'Minuta' or a sport of 'Minuta'.

FIGURE 8. *The oldest known specimen of* Tsuga canadensis *'Minuta' at Harold Epstein's garden in Larchmont, New York. Mr. Epstein obtained the plant prior to 1946 from George Ehrle. It is 18 inches high and 22 inches across. Photo by Gus Kelley, 1983.*

5

Summary

The unbelievably complicated situation described in the last four chapters can be summarized as follows: 'Minuta' was found in the 1930s by an unknown person, probably near the collecting site Daniel St. George discovered in Richmond, Vermont, in 1928. This plant was presented to the horticultural world in 1935 by George Ehrle and Henry Teuscher. Although Ehrle originally received two plants in 1934, he succeeded in propagating only one of them. This plant, which went on to become the 'Minuta' of commerce, died in 1943.[4]

'Abbott's Pigmy Hemlock' was found in May 1933 by Frank Abbott in Richmond, near where 'Minuta' was probably found. It is distinguishable from 'Minuta' by virtue of having its needles arranged in a single plane. The plant was first described by Jenkins as Abbott's #4. In

---

[4]C. F. Jenkins wrote an obituary for the original 'Minuta' in *The Hemlock Arboretum Bulletin* #43 (July 1, 1943): "... he [George Ehrle] has sent three younglings of a specimen he was particularly interested in, *Tsuga canadensis* var. *minuta*. The parent plant which he had growing in a concealed rock garden, overlooking a little pool, had just died. Alas!"

Swartley's 1939 thesis, it was listed as #1349, and was classified under variety *minuta*. The plant was first validly named 'Abbott's Pigmy Hemlock' by Jenkins in 1948. It has never been widely cultivated, and may even be lost to cultivation altogether.

'Pygmaea' has a more confusing history than the other two plants. In the Swartley thesis, mention was made of a plant similar to 'Abbott's Pigmy Hemlock' that had been found with it, but which had died prior to 1939. In 1948, Swartley changed this story, stating that the 'Abbott's Pigmy Hemlock' companion was alive and well, and that it looked just like 'Minuta'. As near as I can tell, it was this unnamed, resurrected companion that went on to become the 'Pygmaea' that was distributed by Joseph Gable in 1941 and first published by Harold Hillier in 1964.

One should not allow the convoluted history of *Tsuga canadensis* 'Minuta' to obscure the fact that the plant is very beautiful and very useful. As a specimen in the alpine or rock garden it has few, if any, rivals in terms of toughness or reliable dwarfness. If this wasn't the case, I never would have written this book, and I certainly wouldn't have planted one in my front yard.

6

Nomenclature

When Henry Teuscher described *'Minuta'* for the first time, he treated it as a true botanical variety:

> This form probably falls under Beissner's *Tsuga canadensis compacta nana,* which, however, is not very well defined by Beissner's description. Because of its proven ability to breed true from seeds, it seems to be worthwhile to distinguish it by a new name, for which var. *minuta* is herewith proposed. Its description may be given as follows: A dwarf compact plant of somewhat irregular shape, but about as broad as it is high. Annual increase in growth not more than 1 cm. The oldest plant of this form which is known and which produces cones and fertile seeds is estimated to be well over fifty years old but does not reach more than 2 feet in height. Its needles—1 to 1.5 mm broad and 6 to 10 mm long—are dark green above and marked with two conspicuous white lines beneath. This variety breeds true from seeds (p. 275).

As far as Teuscher was concerned, the existence of the mother plant and all the babies made 'Minuta' a botanical variety. But this story is not corroborated by St. George, or anyone else for that matter. Even Harold Epstein's 'Minuta', after more than 40 years in cultivation, has not produced a single cone, nor have any other specimens of 'Minuta' that I have seen or asked anyone about. This lack of fertility when coupled with the fact that the proper 'Minuta' of commerce is descended from George Ehrle's *one* surviving plant, clearly suggests that the cultivar name 'Minuta' would be a more appropriate description of the situation than the botanical rank var. *minuta* that Teuscher initially proposed or the forma *minuta* that Alfred Rehder suggested in his bibliography. These Latin classifications are more appropriately used to describe the variation occurring within a population of wild plants, than the variation shown by a single individual.

'Abbott's Pigmy Hemlock' is, of course, very different from 'Minuta' and should not be classed with it. All of the plants that I have seen labelled 'Abbott's Pigmy Hemlock' are 'Minuta'-like in character. I have never seen one that looked like Swartley's original 1939 photo, or matched his or Jenkins's written description. Whether the real 'Abbott's Pigmy Hemlock' is lost to cultivation, or even deserves to be cultivated, remains to be seen. The fact that Jenkins had this specimen at the Hemlock Arboretum labelled as 'Minuta' at least until 1948 suggests that the plant might turn up under that name as well.

'Pygmaea' presents a more complicated situation. In the first place, one can't say for sure where the plant came from. Clearly it should *not* be considered synonymous with 'Abbott's Pigmy Hemlock' as Humphrey Welch suggested in 1977. If anything it should be reduced to synonymy

NOMENCLATURE

with 'Minuta'. Certainly Jenkins and Swartley both implied this when they decided to name only one of the two plants Abbott found—the one that was distinct from 'Minuta'. The correctness of their decision is substantiated by the fact that I could not separate 'Minuta' from 'Pygmaea' by either growth rate or needle length. Really, what one has are two plants that, were it not for their labels, would be impossible to tell apart.

To make matters worse, there is also a problem with the actual name 'Pygmaea'. According to the *International Code of Nomenclature for Cultivated Plants,* cultivar names published on or after 1 January 1959 "must" be a vernacular name, not a botanical name in Latin form (Article 27). Since 'Pygmaea' is a Latin form name that was not published until 1964, it is clearly invalid as far as the *Code* is concerned.

Poor 'Pygmaea', as well as being of uncertain origin and inaccurately described, is improperly named. All one can do in such a situation is to recommend that the name 'Pygmaea' as used by Spingarn in 1969 be dropped, and that the plant so described be referred to as 'Minuta' from now on. Henry Teuscher's original description is certainly broad enough to accommodate both plants.

This lumping of morphologically indistinguishable plants of uncertain origin is well within the rules laid down in the *Cultivated Code—1980,* which makes it clear that a cultivar can consist of "... one clone or several closely similar clones which have a habit of growth which is clearly distinguishable from the normal habit and which is retained by appropriate methods of propagation" (Article 11e).

7

St. George

In all the shuffle over who did what, where, it is easy to lose sight of Daniel M. St. George, the man who, while he did not discover 'Minuta' itself, discovered the spot where it probably came from (figure 9). Born May 31, 1890, Dan was one of nine children. His parents were farmers who moved to Vermont after migrating up the Hudson River from New York State. Longevity seems to run in the St. George line, as Dan's father lived to be 100 and his grandfather to be 113. I tape recorded an interview with him on April 11, 1981. He died two years later in June 1983, at the age of 93.

St. George lived a full life and accomplished many things. During World War I he served in the U.S. Navy and was stationed in Scotland. After the war he collected plants for various Vermont nurseries. During the "slump" he raised raspberries and afterwards served as game warden for J. Watson Webb, a railroad man from Shelburne, Vermont. Mr. Webb owned an estate on Long Island that St. George collected plants for. Dan was also a breeder and seller of lilies and was particularly proud of his *Lilium regale* hybrid, 'Pride of Charlotte', which he developed along with his friend and neighbor, Larry Root.

FIGURE 9. *Daniel M. St. George, 1890–1983.*
Photo by P. Del Tredici, 1981.

ST. GEORGE AND THE PYGMIES

In the course of my interview, St. George talked about his plant collecting activities in general. It turns out he collected mainly native orchids from Vermont bogs and swamps. He specialized in the yellow lady slipper, *Cypripedium calceolus* and its varieties *parviflorum* and *pubescens*. He also collected trilliums and other wild perennials.

"When did you stop collecting?" I asked him. "When the beavers got so damn thick they flooded the old swamps. Killed all the trees and everything else in there. Weren't nothing left to collect that I wanted to collect. They were all flooded out."

St. George also collected tree seedlings. These he pulled up bare-root in between the time when the frost left the ground and the buds started to swell. During the nineteen-twenties, he was paid $10.00 per thousand plants for hemlock, red cedar, balsam and white cedar. Some of his orders were very large, such as the one for 100,000 hemlocks from a Shelburne nursery.

Besides the hemlocks, the only other dwarf plant St. George found was a white cedar variant (*Thuja occidentalis*) which he sold to J. Watson Webb, who planted it on his Long Island estate.

The pyramidal hemlock that still grows in St. George's front yard is a beautiful and very distinctive tree. I have propagated it from cuttings and have received permission from his family to name it 'St. George' in his honor. It was three feet tall in 1932 when he discovered it, and after 50 years in cultivation it is ten feet tall—a growth rate of 1.7 inches a year. It is clearly a hardy, steady grower and a reliably compact plant. *Tsuga canadensis* 'St. George' would make a beautiful addition to any garden (figure 2, page 17).

BIBLIOGRAPHY

Abbey, F. 1967. "Fifty Years with Lilies." *The Lily Yearbook of the North American Lily Society* 20: 112–120.

Brickell, C. D., et al. 1980. "International Code of Nomenclature for Cultivated Plants—1980." *Regnum Vegetabile*, Vol. 104.

Den Ouden, P. and B. K. Boom. 1965. *Manual of Cultivated Conifers*. Martinus Nijhoff, The Hague.

Gotelli, W. T. 1960. "The Gotelli Arboretum of Dwarf and Slow Growing Conifers." *The American Horticultural Magazine* 39(4): 185–198.

Hillier, H. G. 1964. *Dwarf Conifers*. Alpine Garden Society, London; The Scottish Rock Garden Club, Midlothian.

Jenkins, C. F. 1932–1951. *The Hemlock Arboretum Bulletins*. Germantown, Pennsylvania.

Kelsey, H. P. and W. A. Dayton. 1942. *Standardized Plant Names*. Second Edition. J. Horace McFarland Co., Harrisburg, Pa.

Nearing, G. G. 1957. "Nature Can Protect Small Seedlings." *American Rhododendron Society Bulletin* 11(4): 197–199.

Rehder, A. 1949. *Bibliography of Cultivated Trees and Shrubs*. The Arnold Arboretum, Jamaica Plain, Massachusetts.

Spingarn, J. W. 1965. "Canadian Hemlock Variants." *The American Horticultural Magazine* 44(2): 99–101.

———. 1969. "A Few New Forms of *Tsuga canadensis*." *American Rock Garden Society Bulletin* 27(3): 85–90.

Swartley, J. C. 1938. "The Eastern Hemlock and Its Varieties." *The National Nurseryman* 46(6): 4, 10–11.

———. 1939. "Canada Hemlock and its Variations." Master's Degree Thesis, Cornell University.

———. 1946. "A Swing Around the Hemlock Circle." *American Nurseryman* 83(7): 7–10; 83(8): 11–13.

Teuscher, H. 1935. "*Tsuga canadensis minuta* (var. *nova*)." *The New Flora and Sylva* 7(4): 274–275.

———. 1949. "Abbott's Pigmy Hemlock." *Plants and Gardens* 5(3): 141.

Welch, H. J. 1966. *Dwarf Conifers: A Complete Guide*. Charles T. Branford Co., Newton, Massachusetts.

———. 1979. *Manual of Dwarf Conifers*. Theophrastus, Little Compton, Rhode Island.

Yerex, C. and E. L. Kline. 1961. "The Story of the Aurelian Hybrids." *The Lily Yearbook of the North American Lily Society* 14: 54–60.